Hold on to Your Hat, Noddy

HarperCollins *Children's Books*

It was a very windy day
in Toy Town.
The wind was blowing paper around.

Noddy drove to Big-Ears' house.

They were going fishing.

"It is too windy to go out on
the lake," said Big-Ears.
"It is too windy to go out at all!"

Big-Ears told Noddy
that a bird's nest
was blocking his chimney.
He can't light a fire
to warm the house up.

Noddy decided
to cheer up Big-Ears.
He rushed out
just as the wind blew soot
right down the chimney!

The wind has blown Tessie Bear's
knitting bag up like a balloon,
and it is pulling her along!
Noddy offered her a lift in his car.

The wind tugged
at Tessie Bear's hat.

Noddy told her about Big-Ears
and his chimney.
"Can you think of a way
to cheer up Big-Ears?"
Noddy asked.

Tessie Bear said a party
would be a good idea.
"Brilliant," said Noddy.
"We'll give him a surprise party!"

Noddy and Tessie walked around town,
inviting all their friends
to the party at Big-Ears' house.

11

Everyone said they will bring
something for the party.
Tessie Bear and Noddy
decided to take balloons.

Noddy and Tessie Bear drove
to Dinah Doll's stall
to buy the balloons.

Dinah Doll was very excited
about the party.
She gave Noddy
a handful of balloons.

Noddy and Tessie Bear

set off for Big-Ears' house.

On the way, Noddy's car

ran out of petrol, and stopped!

"We're going to miss
Big-Ears' party," said Noddy.
But Tessie Bear had an idea.

Noddy and Tessie Bear
blew up the balloons
and tied them to the car.
The wind pulled them along,
like a sailing boat!

19

The more the wind blew,
the faster the car went.
Noddy tried to use the brake,
but the car lifted off the ground!

The wind lifted the car up into the sky!

The car rose higher and higher!

Noddy and Tessie Bear looked down
at Toytown.

It looked very small.

Suddenly, Noddy had an idea.
They used one of Tessie Bear's
knitting needles to burst
some of the balloons.

24

The car began to come down.

Everybody was having a lovely time
at Big-Ears' party.

Then a loud noise on the roof
made them jump!

Everyone rushed outside

to see what had happened.